COPYRIGHT

TABLE OF CONTENTS

CHAPTER 1

INTRODUCTION TO EXCEL

Many offices and organizations make use of excel application to conduct basic work tasks. So, before you can apply for job in most organizations, you must have knowledge of excel. This software called excel is one of the most used software in the world today. You can create tools, calculators and simulations with excel, and you can create professional reports and dashboard with nice looking charts and visualization.

Excel is great and it is something you will use as professional and in personal life dealings. I remember vividly in my college days when I have no understanding about what Excel is all about. I had a friend called Jason, who is genius in excel applications. During a lunch time, he would call me, and he brought out his laptop and start teaching me some tasks in excel. I became interested because of his interesting teachings.

So, I had to get my own laptop because during that time I was only making use of my mum's own to do some personal work. But because of Jason's teaching, I need to get one laptop for myself so that I could easily understand what he was teaching me. Thanks to my dad who saw sense in what I told him because he was the one that gave me the money I used in purchasing it plus my little savings.

After I got my own laptop, I became more interested in learning the tips and tricks of excel which Jason help me to understand. Here I am today, seeing excel as a minor challenge. So, in this guidebook, I will cover some areas which will help you in your Microsoft excel use. Most of the common business level uses Microsoft excel for business analysis, performing reports, managing human resources and so on.

At a basic level, Microsoft excel is for storing information, analyzing, sorting, and reporting. It extremely popular in business because spreadsheets are highly visual and easy to use. Microsoft adds new features in their newer versions of excel. They are several new features which were added to their latest excel version called Excel 365.

Microsoft Excel in Detail
Some people do not have the knowledge of Microsoft Excel, or what it is used for? The first day I had of excel, I never knew what it was all about until my friend Jason explained it better to me. And since then, I fell in love with Microsoft Excel. So, in this section I will explain it in detail so that you can have a full knowledge about it.

What does Microsoft Excel mean?
Microsoft Excel is a software program organized by Microsoft cooperation that allows users to organize, format and calculates data with formulas using a spreadsheet. This software first appeared on the

scene back in 1987, and since then it has grown to become one of the most popular software for home and business.

The spreadsheet contains number of columns and rows, where each intersection of a row and column makes a cell. Each cell does contain one point of information.

Excel is commercial spreadsheet application produced and distributed by Microsoft for Microsoft Windows and Mac OS X. Its basic features are to perform some calculations, using graphing tools, create pivot tables, and create micro programming language. Excel has great features as every other spreadsheet, which use a collection of cells arranged into columns and rows to organize data. They also display data as charts, histograms and line graphs.

Excel allows users to insert data so as to view various factors from different perspective. Virtual Basic is used for application in Excel, allowing users to create variety of complex numerical methods. Programs are given an option to code directly using the virtual Basic editor, including window for writing code, debunking and code module organization.

What is Microsoft Excel Used For?

Microsoft Excel is a software which is mostly use by lot of individuals in daily activities because it helps in saving time and always gives correct calculations. Excel is been used for several years now and always get upgraded every occasionally. What makes me like excel is that it is anywhere in any kind of job. It is compulsory to learn how to operate it because the world currently is all about digital.

One can store data in excel in a form of charts and spreadsheet. You can access your Microsoft Excel anywhere, you can as well work on excel with your Android phone or iPhone. Excel has become exceptional package for years now because so many of work can be done with it.

It will interest you to know that Microsoft Excel provides security to your files so that it will not get damage. And with your Microsoft account, you can also keep your password protected.

Excel is used to organize various data and perform mathematical calculations. Microsoft Excel is used in various business organization around the world both small and large companies.

Excel are used in data entry, accounting, financial analysis, task management, programming, customer relationship management, time management and so many others.

Reasons Why You need to Learn Microsoft Excel Skill
Learning how to operate Excel is extremely good. If you know how to work with excel, you will have higher chances of being employed. Most people loss their dream jobs today because they are not expert in Microsoft Excel. No knowledge is waste, so you need it. If you know how to use excel today, you will always be in safer hand when going for interview. Having excel skill can make you an asset to any company.

Microsoft Excel Terminology

Knowing the terms used in excel is knowing the possibilities in excel. It is going to be an interesting fact if you know how to use excel but for those who do not have much knowledge of excel but are interested in learning, the rewards for mastering how to use excel is much. Though the beginning may be little bit stressful because you might get lost in spreadsheet jargon and you might get confused, I will be teaching you some common terminologies you are likely to come in contact with for easy understanding.

Worksheet

Worksheet which is also known as spreadsheet is a collection of cells organize in rows and columns that you can enter data into. Each worksheet contains 1048576 rows and 16384 columns. It is possible to have multiple worksheets nestled in a workbook, but only one of the worksheets is active at a time. Tab at the bottom part of the worksheet will indicate which worksheet you are currently working on and it is often referred to as active sheets. Worksheet serves as a giant table that allows you to organize information.

Workbook

A workbook is a document which contains one or more spreadsheet/worksheet where you can organize your data. The workbook can be created from a blank template.

Columns, Rows and Cells

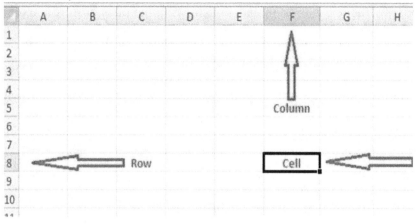

Fig 1: Column, row and cell in picture

Columns run vertically across the worksheet. Columns are cells arranged in a vertical order. They range from A to XFD. Excel platforms make use of columns and rows to display information. Columns are identify using letters of alphabets (A, B, C etc.) and run across the top of the worksheet.

Rows

Row is a horizontal section across the spreadsheet which contain many cells. And in all spreadsheet programs including Microsoft Excel, rows are labelled using Numbers (1, 2,3 and so on).

Cells

Cells are small rectangular boxes in the worksheet where you input data. A cell is the intersection of a row and column. Every worksheet is made up of a thousand of cells. It is identified by row number and column header such as A1, A2. Each cell has its own name or cell address based on its column and row.

Formula Bar

Formula bar is a tool bar located at the top of Microsoft Excel worksheet window with a formula FX next to it. It is used to enter or copy an existing formula into cells or charts. For example, if you are typing a formula in the cells of your worksheet, you will discover that the formula does not only appear on the cell, but it also appears at the formula bar.

Copy, Cut and Paste

I know that these words are not new to you. In Microsoft application, copy, paste and cut are frequently used. So, in this teaching I will use this term frequently.

Copy is used when you want to copy a data. That is if it is by default when you copy (or cut) and paste in excel, everything in the source cell or range—data, formatting, formulas, validation, comments—is pasted to the destination cell(s). This is what happens when you press CTRL+V to paste.

Formatting

Learning how to format documents in excel is essential. When we format some cell in excel, it will change the appearance of the number without changing the number itself.

One cell can be formatted by highlighting one cell at a time or you can format all the cells in excel by highlighting all the cells at once. When you are done highlighting the require cells you wish to format, then, choose your formatting option from the Home tab.

They are extremely two most useful ways which you can use to format cell in excel. To format a cell in excel, you can click on the Home tab or you can right-click to select the format cell from drop-down menu. But using Home tab to format your desire text is a nice choice for beginners in excel. There are several short ways cell can be formatted which I will also discuss about such as using CTRL+B for bold, CTRL+I for italics and so on.

Click

Click is an action of pressing a mouse button. So, if I ask you to click, what I simply mean is to use your mouse and locate a place where you want to input a data, or type something with the help of arrow and right click or left click on the option so that you can carry on your task.

Data

In this my teaching, I will always use the term data. When I mention data in any category, just bear this in mind that am referring to text, icons or numbers.

What are the Uses of Microsoft Excel in Our Daily Life?

Nowadays, there are different devices used for calculations and excel happens to be the best of all. Performing calculations with excel format has been a good choice for years now because it makes calculations simple and accurate at all time. That is why different companies in the world do make use of excel in their daily activities. Excel helps people to do calculations in no time.

Microsoft Excel is the most popular spreadsheet software in the world today. Every organization, companies and individuals do make use of excel because it is used to perform different tasks. Millions of people do use excel. So, if you do not learn how to use excel now, this simply means you may be lagging.

Let me mention different places excel can be use:

1. Education.

In education system, there are different uses of excel. Microsoft Excel has made teaching to be easier for teachers. Many teachers use excel in their teaching such as tables, shapes and other important tools from excel to present the topics to students. Also, teachers use formulas to teach some mathematical calculations. The data visualization of Microsoft Excel is a key to teachers. Microsoft Excel is also used in education system to create timetable for students. They are prebuilt templates in Microsoft Excel which is used to create timetable. Microsoft excel versions have different formulas that can be used in educational system.

2. Business.

Excel is playing important role in business. Almost all the business organizations are making use of excel. The use of excel in business organization varies. Both large organization and small organizations relies on excel to be able to carry out their daily tasks. Businesses do use excel to carry out goal setting, budgeting process, planning and so on.

Microsoft Excel does offer IF formulas, which is very helpful in creating hundreds of logics in the business calculations. Microsoft Excel is good for business operations. And all you need to do is to visit template and take a good advantage of it. The best part of prebuilt templates is that you do not need to create anything from scratch.

3. Goal Setting and Planning

We all have different goals about using Excel. We can use Microsoft Excel to perform and manage different tasks in our daily activities. when ever we complete daily tasks, we write on remark columns that we are done with the task.

4. Business Owners

I have explained to you the uses of Excel in business. Now, we are going to deal on business owners. Business owners need excel. Some tasks which business owners perform are team management, work progress, pay-outs detail and all these requires excel before they can be performed.

5. Housewives

You might be wondering what housewives have to do with excel application. Like I mentioned before, everybody can make use of excel and having the knowledge of excel will help you in all areas of life. Excel helps housewives to manage some house daily expenses as well as grocery. With the use of excel, one can create the report for weekly or monthly expenses. Most of the housewives do use excel to teach their children some basic skills.

6. Data Analysis and Data Science

Data analysis is one of the emerging fields in business perspective. The business needs to perform different activities of data because companies are not using a single source. They do use multiple sources such as their blog, e-commerce site, their social media, offline data and lots more. All these jobs need a lot of time and energy to perform. Sometimes, it becomes difficult for some businesses to handle such data.

7. Daily Progress Report

In daily progress report, excel plays a better role. Most of the companies track the weekly expenses with daily progress report in excel. In project-based companies, some clients need weekly progress report from the company because of this reason. Some companies always make a daily progress report to the client so that they can showcase the daily work progress. Excel do provide table with date and time of the action.

8. Carrier Development

In career development, Microsoft Excel plays a major role. Microsoft Excel teaches you the most powerful skills of management. You can do your calculations with the help of excel.

The more you learn excel, the more successful you will become. If you develop your excel skill to the peak level, you are eligible to get a nice job for yourself.

How to get Microsoft Excel Application

Getting Microsoft Excel for your device is not a big task at all. Microsoft Excel can be bought with money and for free. I will walk you through on the processes. These are procedures you can use to get access to Microsoft Excel.

1. You can buy and install office software to your computer

2. You can access Microsoft Excel for free

3. With the use of iPhone and Android phone, you can as well get access to it

How to install and download Microsoft office

I will teach you how to install and download Microsoft office whether is office 2010, 2013, 2016, 2019, or Microsoft 365. We still have office 2007 but Microsoft office does not support it any longer. Through this teaching, I will teach you how you can install and download it through an official channels of Microsoft office. To use this package for free, you will have an office 365 subscription or product key so that you can use this software.

There is Microsoft office Online which includes some popular programs such as Word, Excel, and PowerPoint and they are free online with limited functionalities. You can vividly recall that in the past years you can only have access to Word, Excel or PowerPoint either in the Play Store or App Store but few months back Microsoft office announced the Office app. The Office app is now available at Playstore or App store.

You might be wondering what Office app does. The office app combines the three apps into one. The benefits of this Office app are that it gives enough of space and a lot of efficiency. Having Microsoft Excel for free is a new development from Microsoft cooperation which enables you to have access to this application without paying for it. We have different channels which you can use to install your Microsoft office:

1. On your PC, at browser box, to get the office, type in www.office.com or www.microsoft.com and proceed with other steps I will explain later. There are other channels.

2. It is also accessible at www.amazon.com

3. Walmart which is accessible through www.walmart.com

4. indigo software company at www.indigosoftwarecompany.com. And so many other channels.

Accessing Office via www.microsoft.com

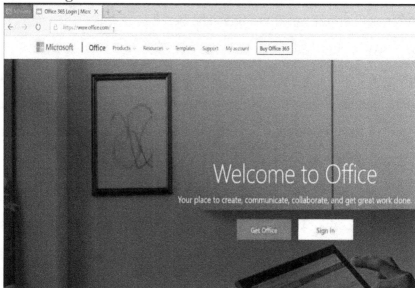

Fig 1.1: The Home view of Microsoft Office website

Once you are on the Homepage of the website, you will see sign in button and get office buttons, click on the sign in. Once it is open, sign in with your Microsoft account details. If you do not have any Microsoft account, sign up for one.

On the top side of the webpage, you will see the Install office button, click on it to install. Once you click on the Install office, it will automatically take you to installation page. Another page will come up asking you the language preference, and so on, input the necessary information in the box provided for you.

But if you are looking for Office 2010, 2019, 2013, you can visit any shop that sells such versions of Office, but and install any of them using the installation guide on the CD cover.

How to Download and Install an Official Microsoft Excel for Mobile Phone for Free

Most times, we may not have our own computer to carry along anywhere we are going, or we may not have our own personal computer that we can use to install excel and learn. Technology have made it possible for us that some of our smart phones can operate excel software. But unfortunately, it might not perform exactly everything you might wish but I can assure you that some high-quality phones can take up the tasks to the best level.

In this my teaching, I will teach you step by step procedures on how you can download the application on your phones.

Step 1

Visit Play store in your mobile phone and type Microsoft Excel in the search box.

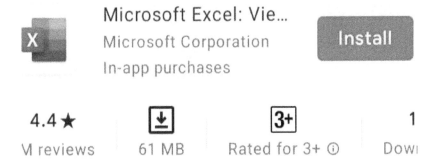

Fig1.2: Microsoft Excel on Play Store

Step 2

Click on the **Install** button as shown in the picture above.

Step 3

After installing and downloading the application, go to your phone and click the application to open it.

CHAPTER 2

SOME BASIC TASKS IN EXCEL

If you are a complete user of excel or you never used it before or if you are genius in Excel and you want to know some new format in excel, this book is for you. I have explained how you can get Microsoft Excel and I know by now you have installed it to your desktop computer. The difference between purchased Microsoft Office and free Microsoft Office is that the purchased one have a lot of features than the free one. If you have already installed your Microsoft office. Then, it is time for us to work on excel spreadsheet.

How to Get Access to Your Excel Worksheet
With your desktop computer, click on the excel on the task bar or search for it in your computer via the Start button and click on it to open. When you open it, you will see something like this photo shown below.

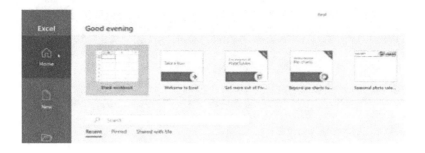

Fig 2: Home screen of excel

At the home screen, you will see numbers of template. Also, you will be shown Blank workbook. Excel has a good number of sheet templates you can work on and if you want more you can click on **More templates**. Click on the first template to start your data entry. The data can be text or numbers and you can still insert tables and charts.

Blank Workbook Explained

A workbook is a file that helps you organize data in worksheet or spreadsheet. The workbook can be created from template or blank workbook.

When blank opens, it is time to enter any data you wish to have inside the Excel. You can create more sheets inside the workbook if you wish for more. At the end of the work, you will need to save all the sheets in one workbook with one file name. But different sheets can bear different names as they are house in a workbook.

How Sheets can be Created in a Single Workbook

Some people do not know that more sheets can be created inside a single file of workbook. Having different sheets in single workbook makes excel package exceptional. I will walk you through on how that can be achieved. It is a simple task to perform. If you are not aware of it just follow this procedure below:

- Use your mouse to click on the blank template I mentioned to you earlier where you want to input your data. Once it is open, check at the bottom part of the worksheet. Where a plus sign (+) is located, click it as shown below:

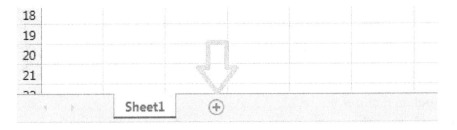

Fig 2.1: Click the (+) to add more sheets

If you want to have extra spreadsheets, keep clicking on the (+). When you create new sheet in excel, it is given default name as sheet 1. You can still copy one of your existence sheets, this will create a new worksheet and duplicate the contents. To copy a Sheets, right click the sheet you want, then select move or copy from the menu tabs.

Check the box that say create a copy and click on the box. And identify where you want the worksheet to go and click Ok and the copy will appear the same way as original one. You can rename it by right clicking the tab and choose Rename. When you are done with the rename, click anywhere at the tab to deselected or press enter on your keyboard. You can still update the sheets by yourself.

You can still recolor the sheet to make them easy for reference. To do this right click the tab to select the tab color.

If you want to delete the worksheet you do not need anymore, you can as well delete them by right clicking the tab and choose Delete.

When you have multiple worksheets, you can work with each one individually or you can add several data at a time. This can be useful if you are working with a lot of data that are closely related.

Basic Tools in Excel and Their Functions

Understanding the basic tools in excel will make your work easy and unique. I am going to teach you some necessary basic tools in excel. Look at pictures below:

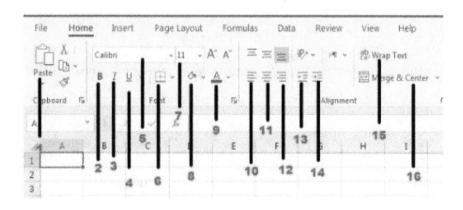

Fig 2.2: Basic tools in excel numbered

Paste (1)

The number 1 tool as shown in the above is Paste. By default, when you copy (cut) and Paste in excel, everything in the source cell or range-data, formulas, formatting, validation, comments- is pasted to the destination cell(s). And this action of paste can also be conducted when you press CTRL+V after selecting a cell. All you needed to do as a user is that you need to click at the cell you want to paste on then click on the Paste tool and the data will be inserted at the appropriate cell.

Apply Bold (2), Italic (3) and Underline (4)

The number 2, 3, 4 of fig 2.2: stands for bold, Italic, and underline respectively. Bold is a frequently used tool used in Microsoft Excel. It is used to make letters thicker than they appear in the initial time and you can use it to attract the interest of a reader.

Italic is number 3 labelled above which is used to draw the attention of the reader at one spot. The word italics always appear in fashionable way like the word *gold.*

Underline is number 4 which is used to separate some text from another. As the name sounds, it is used to underline text in a cell.

How You can Make Number or text Bold, Italics or Underline in Excel
You can make your text or number bold, italic or underline by

1. Select the text or number you want to format.

2. Click on the bold, Italic or underline tool in the Home tab.

In addition, the shortcuts for these commands are as follow:

3. To make your texts or number bold press CTRL+B.

4. For italics press CTRL+I.

5. To underline your text or number press CTRL+U.

The bold, italics and underline buttons on the formatting toolbar in excel are like toggle switches: click once to turn on, click again to turn it off.

Border in excel (6)

In this my teaching, am going to teach you how you can border cells in excel by using predefined options and how you can still create your custom border style. Adding border in excel can help you to distinguish different sections, emphasize certain data such as columns heading or rows and make your work look presentable. Without borders, excel worksheet can be difficult to read because of complex structure. A border is a line around a cell. The cell border is used to accent specific sections of spreadsheet to make it stand out.

Border and worksheet gridlines look similar, but border is ticker. Border do not appear by default; you need to apply it manually.

How Border can be Created
The fastest way border can be applied in Excel is to:

1. Select a cell or range of cells you want to border, on the **Home** tab, in the **Font** group, click the arrow next to border button and the list of borders will pop up.

2. Click on the border you wish to apply, and it will be added to the cell immediately.

Fonts in Excel

If you change fonts of your text, it will make your worksheets easier to read and look more professional to your reader. You might be wondering what font, or the fonts size is. Font which is number 5 in Fig 2.2 is the style you give to a text or character. While the fonts size which is number 7 in the above table is the size you give to your texts or characters.

The fonts and fonts size of excel is commonly used when you want your documents to fit for one document. You can change your full work to small font size or bigger depends on how you want to present your work.

To use the fonts or the font size take the following steps below.

1. Select the text or character you wish to change.

2. On the Home tab, click on the font size if you want to change the size of the text or click on the font if you want to change the style of the text.

3. When you choose the font or the size, hit Enter key on your computer keyboard.

Fill Color (8) and Font Color (9)

The number 8 tool in the picture is called Fill color. Fill color is a tool in excel spreadsheet used in changing the background color of cells. To perform this tasks, use your mouse to select the particular cell you want to change the color, once you are done selecting them click on the fill color tool and select the desire color you wish to have from the color gallery.

Font color is used to change the color of the text or characters.

Align left (10), Center Align (11) and Right Align (12)

With Microsoft Excel, cell alignment is how your text or number are being positioned in the cell. By default, text that is within a cell is left-aligned and bottom-aligned. But sometimes, you might want to align your text either in the center or on the right. Microsoft Excel has made that possible. You can align your text in any way you wish to have it.

The align-left aligns the contents along the edge of the cell and align-center puts the contents in the middle of the cell. Also, the align-right puts the contents along the right edge of the cell.

If you want to Align any text or number, just select the text and click on the align tools at Home tab and select which side you want your text to be. The first row of the align option have top align, middle align, and bottom align. You can choose one of these three options for your cell. The second row of the align section contains left-align, center and right-aligned. You can choose one of these three options for your cell in excel for example.

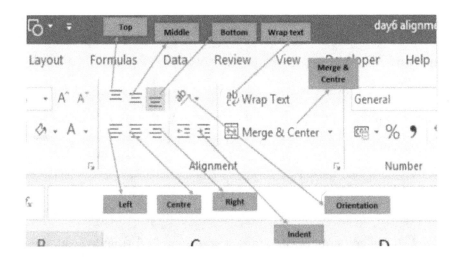

Fig 2.3: Alignment commands with other commands indicated

Decrease Indent (12) and Increase Indent (13)

The number 12 of Fig 2.2 stands for Decrease Indent. This tool enables you to move the text in cell closer to the cell border. The Increase Indent which is labelled 13 in Fig 2.2 enables you to move text in a cell farther away from the cell border.

Step to Step Guide on How to Decrease or Increase Indent in a Cell

If you want to indent the contents of a cell, you must use excel dedicated increase button.

1. The first step you will take is to select the cell containing the information you want to indent.

2. Click on the Increase or Decrease Indent in the **Home** tab.

Wrap Text

The command number 15 stands for Wrap Text command. Wrapping text in cell makes it easier to view all the data in that cell. Wrap Text is used to position text in all the cell to show that all the text entered appropriately.

How Text can be Wrapped in Excel
To use wrap text command in excel, take these steps:

1. Select the cell containing the text you want to format in worksheet.

2. Click on the **Wrap Text** command at the **Home** tab. You can as well select the cell and press the shortcut **Alt + H + W**.

Cells Merge Style

The number 16 is known as cells merge style. The cells merge style tool is used to merge different cells in worksheet as one. To merge cells, first select the cells you want to merge. The next step is to click **Merge Styles**. From the list of merge options that will be displayed, select one, example is **Merge & Center**.

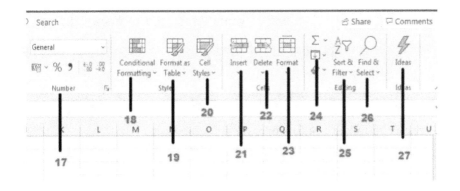

Fig 2.4: Second part of the basic tools in excel located in the **Home** tab

Number Group (17)

The category labelled number 17 stands for Number group. Number is a group name. It contains many mathematical and statistical symbols such as percent, accounting symbols and so on. The accounting symbols is used to show different number of currencies such as Euro and Dollars in a number placement. If you want to see the accounting tool, use your cursor to select the cell. Once you are done with the selection, click on the Accounting symbol tool to select the currency you like to assign to the number. If you want to assign other tools, follow the same step.

Conditional Formatting (18)

The number 18 of Fig 2.4 stands for Conditional Formatting tool. Conditional Formatting is a feature in new excel spreadsheet versions which apply specific formatting to cells that meet certain criteria. It is used as color-based formatting to highlight, emphasize, or differentiate among data and information stored in a spreadsheet. If you want to see the function of the tool in a spreadsheet, select the cells containing some data, example numbers. Click on the Home tab and select the conditional formatting tool. Among the option shown, select any required option for your selected data.

Format as Table (19)

The number 19 of above fig 2.4 stands for Format as Table command. In excel, when format as table is used, it will automatically convert your data range to table. You can format the cell in a worksheet into table with this tool.

Cell Styles (20), Insert (21), Delete (22) and Format (23)

The number 20 stands for cell styles. It is used to choose the style of any cell you want to use. And number 21 stands from Insert command and it is used to insert sheets, rows, columns and cells.

The number 22 of Fig 2.4 stands for Delete. It is used to delete unwanted data from the cells. You can use it to delete row, columns and cells. To perform the task of cell deleting for instance, click on the Home tab of your workbook and select the cell you wish to delete. Click on the Delete tool and complete the action. The number 23 stands for Format. The format is used to change the size of cell, hide and unhide, organize sheets and protection of workbook.

Number 24: Sum Symbols, Fill and Clear Commands

The number 24 stands for Sum symbol, Fill and Clear commands. Each one has its own function to perform. The sum symbol is used to solve mathematical problems. To perform this task of sum, highlight the numbers in different cells, click the Sum symbol and select Sum from the options. You can also find the average of numbers, minimum and maximum from this command. Just select the option that best fit into what you want to do, and the answer will be delivered.

The fill command is used to fill in data into adjacent range of cells. To perform this task of fill, highlight the cell containing the data you wish to fill and select fill option.

Clear as the name sounds is used in removing the text, number and formulas you initially inserted in cells of excel spreadsheet. To perform this task of clear, select the cell containing any text, click Clear tool and select any option from the list.

Number 25: Sort & Filter

Sort & Filter command in Microsoft Excel is for editing feature. This tool is for sorting and filtering of document in Excel and it is represented by 25 command.

Excel Sorting and Filtering Data

You can sort out letters or numbers in by writing the names of peoples or numbers in columns. After you are done with the names or numbers, highlight all the cells in the column containing the data you want to sort. The next is click on the Home tab and click on the Sort & Filter command. Select either to sort from A-Z or Sort Smallest to largest depending of the nature of the text you have in the selected cells.

Number 26: Find and Select

This tool is used in finding numbers, text, formulas or notes in a workbook.

Ideas Command (27)

The number 27 stand for Ideas command. This command is new in Microsoft Office newer version. Some older versions do come with it. Ideas in Excel allows you to understand your data through natural language queries which enables you to ask questions about your data without having to write complicated formulas. This command does work with artificial intelligent. The ideas command works with internet which means it can be operated when connected to internet.

How to Change the Display Language in Excel
There may be different reason you may want to change the existing language of your Microsoft Excel to another. Microsoft Excel comes with English language if you select it as you default during installation. I will explain to you how you can change to any other one if you choose to do so.

1. Open your Excel desktop application and click on the File tab.

2. Click on the **Options**, look for **Language** in the dialog box and click on it.

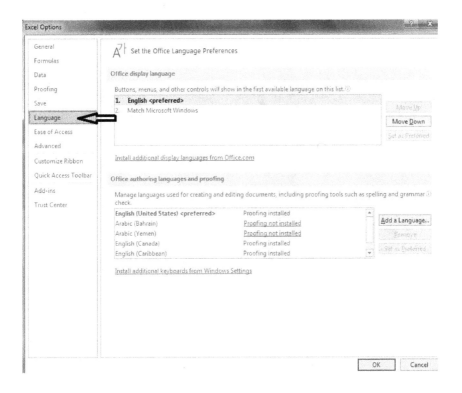

Fig 2.5: Click Language heading as shown in the picture

3. In the list of languages in **Office authoring language and proofing**, check if your required language is there. If the language you want is on the list, click on it, click **Set as Preferred**, and click **Ok** button for it to be save. But if the language you want to change to is not on the group list, click on the **Add a Language** button. You will be shown some languages and from there choose the language you need for excel and it will be added. As the language is added, select it, click **Set as Preferred** and click the **Ok** button.

Note: Changing the excel language to English may enable some features that can be available for the English version only at that moment.

Parts of Excel Interface

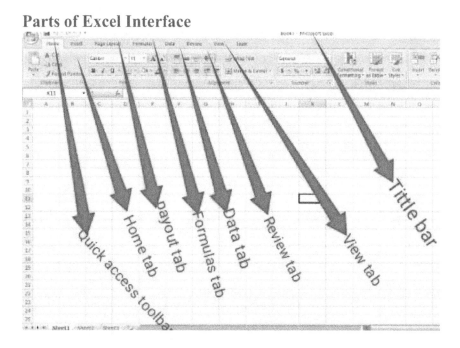

Fig 2.6: Parts of Excel interface in picture

Quick Access Toolbar

The quick access toolbar is located at the top left of the screen. It is used to create a customizable tool bar to easily access commands buttons you used most often. It contains print, undo and redo buttons.

If you want to print any document, instead of going through **File>Print**, you can directly click the print button from quick access toolbar in Excel and get the documents printed (but the position of Print button in quick access toolbar depends on the version of excel you are using).

32

Tittle Bar

The tittle bar is located at the top middle of the screen is your tittle bar. It is used to display the workbook name and programs you are using in excel.

Ribbon Tabs

Ribbon tabs contain group of commands which are related to a central task and one of them is a **Home** tab. The Home tab contains some actions such as formatting, pasting, copying, inserting and deleting columns and rows.

Inserting Tab

The Insert tab contains a lot of commands that will enable you to insert an object such as charts and sheets in the spreadsheet.

Page Layout Tab

The page layout tab holds all the commands that will enable you to determine how your spreadsheet looks when printed. This command control options such as page margins, print area, orientation and paper size, headers and footers, repeated tittle, background and heading.

Formulas Tab

This tab holds all the commands that help define, control all the excel formulas. It is used to insert functions, define the name, create the name range, review the formula etc. It is used to show formula in the sheets.

Data Tab

The data tab contains commands that will enable you connect to external data as well as manage the data from your spreadsheet.

Review Tab

The review tab in excel is used to insert command into cells in a worksheet. This tab can be used to protect sheets, protect workbook and track changes.

View Tab

The commands in view tab are designed to help you control how you can easily interact with your spreadsheet.

Team Tab

The team tab is not visible by default on the Microsoft Excel workbook. You need to install some packages for you to view the team tab and it is mostly use for programming purposes.

Formula Bar

The formula bar in excel is a nice toolbar which is located at the top of the excel worksheet Window with a label (*fx*). It is used to enter formula or copy existing one.

CHAPTER 3

EXCEL ELEMENTS AND FURTHER TASKS

Welcome to a new chapter in excel where I will continue to guide you on the elements that make up excel software. Not only that, I will guide you on how to complete additional functions. I might have touched some things you will see in this chapter, but I want them to sink into you.

What is Excel Ribbon?
I have explained some ribbon tabs in chapter 2 of this book. A ribbon or ribbon panel is the combination of all excel tabs apart from file tab. The ribbon is a part of excel window. It is a part that shows the commands we needed in excel to complete certain tasks.

Microsoft Excel has Many Elements
The elements of Microsoft Excel are as follow:

1. File bar

2. Quick Access Toolbar

3. Ribbon

4. Status Bar

5. Formula Bar

6. Task Pane

Ribbon Components
The following tabs do appear on the ribbon tabs:

- Home tab
- Insert
- Page Layout
- Formulas
- Data
- Review and
- View

How Data can be Enter in a Workbook?
Entering data in a workbook is a simple task to do. But as a beginner, it is my duty to teach you how that can be done. If you have not used excel before, that means this part is for you but if you know how data can be enter in your workbook then no need of reading this subheading. Inputting data in your workbook can be done in this way:

1. Select the cell which you want to input text into.

2. On your keyboard, type any text you wish to have there.

3. When you are done typing the text you want, click outside of the cell or click on another cell.

How to Insert Date and Time in a Cell
Date and time can be easily inserted into your excel workbook. Date and time changing in excel does not require you to check the current date before inserting. When you press key combinations such as Ctrl+;

in order to insert the current date in cell, excel does take a snapshot of current date and then inserts the date in the cell because the cell value does not change. Select the cell which you want to insert the current date and time in the workbook. And follow the following steps:

- Press Ctrl+; (semi-colon) to insert the current date.
- If you want to insert the current time, press Ctrl;(semi-colon), then press Ctrl+Shift+; (semi-colon).
- To be able to insert the current date and time, press Ctrl+;(semi-colon), then press space and press Ctrl+Shift+;(semi-colon).

Change the Date or Time Format
To be able to change the date or time format of excel application, right click on a cell, and select format cells. Then, on the format cells dialog box, in the number tab, under category, click date or time and in the type list, choose a type and click Ok button.

How to Show or Hide Excel Ribbon
Hiding some tabs in excel is possible. Some users like hiding some of the tabs in Excel while some want to hide tabs but do not know how to go about it. You can hide tabs in Excel from the following steps.

- You can change your view and maximize the ribbon by clicking on the **Ribbon Display Options**. It is at the top right corner of excel as shown below:

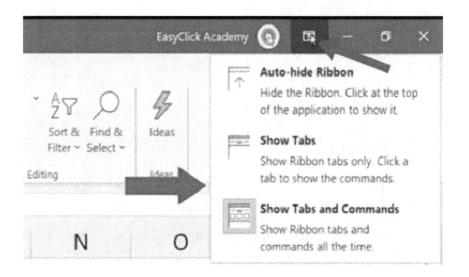

Fig 3: The Ribbon Display Options shown

- A menu will be opened. The menu contains three different options. You can select **Show Tabs and Commands** for the ribbon to show all tabs and full commands. This option provides full access to all the commands. It limits the available space in your workbook. You can press **Ctrl+F1** to show and hide commands in the Ribbon.

- Select the **Show Tabs** ribbon to display on the ribbon tabs without commands.

- Select **Auto-hide Ribbon** to hide all tabs and commands. If you use this option of tabs, you will have a lot of space in the screen of your workbook.

How to Save and Share Excel Document with Save and Share Tools

Saving and sharing of file online is done by OneDrive. The online application has storage space for your documents and files. When you store your documents in OneDrive, you can access them anywhere even if you are not close to your computer.

If you want to use OneDrive for your storage, make sure you log in through excel with your Microsoft account. But if you want to save your excel file in your computer, at the top where quick access toolbar is located, click on the **Save** icon.

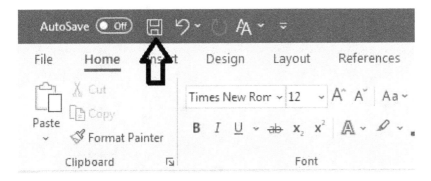

Fig 3.1: The Save icon pointed by arrow

Once the save command menu opens, click on the **Browse**, enter the name you want your file to answer and click **Save**. When you add new data in your spreadsheet, you can occasionally click the Save icon to save them along side with the previously save. But in this new saving, you do not have to pass through the stress of adding new file name.

Another option of Saving a file is that you can use **OneDrive** or **This PC** option in the save file page. You can customize excel to always save your file to **This PC** by default.

If you want to achieve that, these are the steps you need to take:

- Click the **File** tab of the excel application.

- Select Options from the list of options that will be shown to you.

- Click **Save** in the left side of the page in the Excel Options dialog box.

- Check the box Save to Computer by default.

- Click the **Ok** button for your customization to be saved.

Fig 3.2: Picture explains from step 3 to 5

If you ever forget to save or your computer get off when you are working with it, do not worry about it because Auto recovery features saves the backup of your workbook automatically.

To recover an unsaved file, all you are to do is to reopen the excel and the document recovery page will appear. There you will recover all the recovery access of the files.

By default, excel AutoSave features save up every backup copy every 10mins if enabled. So, if you are working on something less than 10mins, you may not be able to use this feature. You can also export your workbook to alternate file type by clicking on the Export on the side page of the field. Exporting as a PDF is a good choice if you want to send your workbook to someone who does not have Excel. This format allows them to view but not adding anything to the workbook.

On under Change File Type, you can access several formats depending on what you need.

To share your workbook with others, click on the share button in the righthand corner of excel.

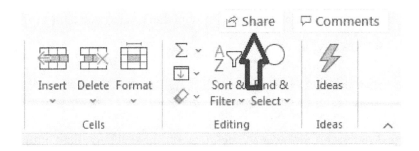

Fig 3.3: The share button in excel

Next, upload your workbook to OneDrive. So, click on the option that is associated with your account, allow to upload. Once it is uploaded, you can email an invitation for others to view or added file.

There are more ways to share at the bottom of the window like attaching the workbook to email or get a shareable link. If you have office 365, you can use AutoSave features once you upload your workbook to OneDrive. Whenever you make a change, it will automatically save your file.

However, if you want to disable this feature, click on the top left corner where AutoSave feature button is located. And if you want to reactivate the Auto saving features, still click on it anytime you want.

How to Delete Sheet in Excel

I will teach you how excel sheet can be deleted. If you do not need one or more spreadsheets in your workbook anymore, you can easily delete them. But you need to take note that once a spreadsheet is deleted from a workbook, you will lose all the data stored in it and you will not be able to retrieve them back. Also, you will not be able to use the data from the deleted spreadsheet to another sheet. So, before you delete any data from your spreadsheet, make sure that it is not useful to you anymore.

You can delete the sheet in excel by selecting it, and right click on the delete tool to delete the sheet. The Excel sheet will drop a notification warning asking you if you want to delete such sheet. Then click on the delete and you are done.

Comment in Excel

A comment in excel is a tool used to add words in the form of comment to excel spreadsheet. The comment tool is located at New Comment Command button on the Ribbon's tab (Alt+RC) or the comment button on the Insert tab (Alt+NC2) or press Shift+F2.

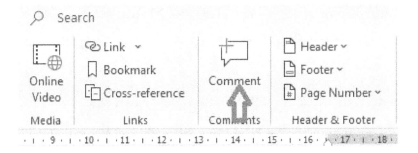

Fig 3.4: The comment tool of excel in Insert tab

When you click the **Comment** tool, a comment text box will appear. This text box does contain name of the user as it appears in the user name text box on the general tab in the excel options dialog box (Alt+FT) and the insertion box is located at the beginning of a new line below the user name. Type in the text you want to have in it and click out.

This comment tool is used when you want to send someone some file, it is a word attached to the file telling the person what to do with already sent file through you. The comment is used when you want to drop some details about a file.

Things to keep in Mind

You are to take note that comments can be edited. Comments in an office documents are stored in the file, so anyone with edit access can edit your comments.

You can add comments to cell. When any Cell has a comment, there will be an indicator at the corner of the cell. When you hover your cursor over the cell, the comment will appear.

Annotate Cell with Note

To add note, right-click the cell and select **New Note**, enter your note. When you are done entering your note, click outside the cell. To see more valuable actions, right-click the cell, you can edit the note, delete or do more through the provided options.

CHAPTER 4

EVALUATION TASKS IN EXCEL

It is important to evaluate tasks in excel. These evaluations can be done through the **Review** tab of excel software. I will first put you through on how to perform few tasks which I did not cover in the previous chapter before going into review in detail.

Select All Explained
One of the problems I do encounter when working with data which I added to my worksheet is the ability to select all the contents in the worksheet at one click. If you want to perform this task, click on the edge part of the worksheet as shown below.

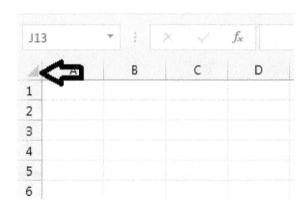

Fig 4: Select All icon pointed by the arrow

The Select All looks like network signal indication found on our mobile phones. Click on that position arrow tab to select all the data in the worksheet. This tool will help you to copy rows and columns of the spreadsheet and allow you to take the data to another spreadsheet. You can use this tool when you want to use paste special-value option to remove any formulas from the spreadsheet. You can be able to select, copy and paste some special values in your worksheet.

How Sheets are Renamed in Workbook
Default sheet name that is located at the down part of your workbook can be rename. You might not like using the default names, such as Sheet1, Sheets 2, Sheet3 etc. You can give your sheets any name you want. So, if you want to give your sheets unique name, follow the following steps:

- At the bottom part of the workbook where sheet1 or Sheet2 is located, right-click the default sheet which you want to change its default name.

Fig 4.1: Options for renaming of sheet.

- Click **Rename** tab
- Type in the new name you want your workbook to answer and tap enter key in your computer keyboard.

Review Tab and What you can Achieve Through it

A Review tab ribbon contains group of commands that can be use to check all the grammar and spelling in a document, track a change in a document, add some certain comments to a document, compare two or more version to a documents or protect a document.

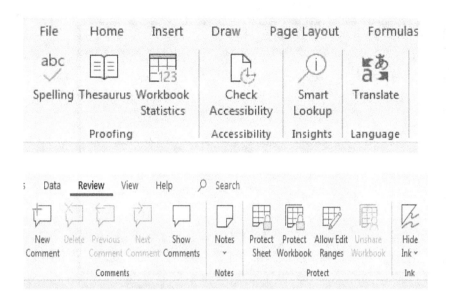

Fig 4.2: Tools in Review tab

The pictures suppose to stand as one but I divided it for you to be able to see the commands available in the review tab clearly to some extent.

Proofing Group in Review Tab
Spelling and grammar

The spelling and grammar command give you room to check any possible error that may occur in your document. To check the spelling or grammar in your document, click the **Review** tab. The next step is click on the **Spelling** button. The check will run through the document and make suggestions are made if any grammatical and spelling errors are discovered.

Thesaurus

It is a tool which suggests words that are like already selected word. If you want to perform this task, select a word, click on the **Review** tab and it will view group which contains **Thesaurus**. Click on it and you will be shown the results immediately.

Workbook Statistics

This command tool is used when you want to find the number of words, character, paragraph and links in a document or excel files. This word count can also be found in the bottom part of the window on excel sheet. If you want to use this tool, click the **Review** tab and select the command **Workbook Statistics**.

Accessibility Group
Check Accessibility

The online features an Accessibility Checker command in Review Tab which help you find accessibility issues with your Microsoft Excel document. Anyway, it is important to recognize that automated accessibility checkers are only capable of detecting some of the issues that can affect the accessibility of your document, even when the accessibility checkers does not find anything wrong. To perform this action, just click on the **Check Accessibility** command.

Insights Group
Smart Lookup

This command gives you room to learn more definition about text that has been selected by viewing the definition, images and other results from online if your computer is connected to internet. To access this tool, click on the command that is close to review tab buttons as shown in the above picture and click on the smart lookup command and you will see information about the word displayed by the right margin of the worksheet. The Define and Explore headings are there. When you click on the Explore, it will give you research result on the selected word.

Language Group
Translate

This tool is used to translate words or paragraph in excel to different languages by using machine translator or bilingual dictionaries. This translate tool works with internet. To translate any text, click the cell containing the text and click the Review Tab, once it is opens, locate the translate button and click on it. Select the required language of your choice.

Language

This tool is used to select the language that the document is to be written in.

Comments Group
New Comment

The **New Comment** is a tool in the **Review** tab. It is used to add comment to any cell. I have explained the process to you before now. To add new comment to a cell, select the cell, click the **New Comment** button and the comment box will appear along the right-side of the document window. Type in your comment and click out when you are done.

Delete

The **Delete** button is used in removing comments from excel document. Select the cell that contains the comment and then click the **Delete** button which is in the Review tab. In the other words, this tool can be used to delete any comments in the workbook by selecting the cell and click Delete. **Previous Comment**

The Previous Comment tool allows you to view previously added comment in a spreadsheet if there is any. To be able to display the previous comment from the document, click the Previous Comment button.

Next Comment

The Next Comment tool takes you to the next comment in your workbook in the worksheet. This command is not active when you do not have more than one comments in your worksheet.

Show Comments

This tool shows all the comments that are in the worksheet. Click the show comment button to display all the comments along the side of the document.

Notes

This tool works like comment. Note can be added in a cell. When you apply note in cell, you will not be able to see it until the note command is clicked.

If you want to add notes in excel workbook, what you will do first is to select the cell where the note will be added;

- Click on the **Notes** command at **Review** tab.
- Select the **New Note** tab.
- Type in your text and click out after you finish typing.

Protect Group
Sheet Protection

The **Sheet Protection** tool in **Review** tab enables the user to protect their worksheet so that another person cannot have access to the available data. To be able to protect your sheets which contains data, click on the **Review** tab and click on the **Sheet protection**. Then insert the password you want to use to lock the spreadsheet and click **Ok** button.

Protect Workbook

The workbook can be protected if you want. The protect workbook tool keeps the data in the workbook safe. The workbook contains different sheets in them. To perform this task, click on the **Protect Workbook** tab and type in the password in the dialog box that shows up and click **Ok**.

Allow Edit Ranges

The Allow Edit Range will allow you to set up password for each cell range and gives you the room for other to do the edit on the ones you want them to edit.

CHAPTER 5

EXCEL CHART

A chart is a tool you can use in excel to communicate data graphically. Charts allow the audience to see the meaning behind the numbers, and they make showing comparisons and trend much easier. In Microsoft Excel, a chart is often referred to as graph. It is a visual representation of data from a worksheet that can bring more understanding to the data than just looking at the numbers. A chart is a powerful tool that allows you to visually display data in a variety of different chart formats such as bar, column, pie, radar charts and so on. Creating of charts in Excel is easy.

Columns chart in Excel

Columns chart in excel is used to compare values across categories by using vertical bars. The columns chart is plotted in columns view that is why it is called columns chart. This columns chart is useful when you want to make comparison, to see progress toward a goal, percentage contribution, the distribution of data and actuals against target scenarios. You can create a columns chart in a few clicks.

To plot this chart in your worksheet, follow below steps:

1. Prepare your chart data in your spreadsheet.

2. Select the data.

3. Click on the **Insert** tab and click on the See All charts button as indicated in the picture below:

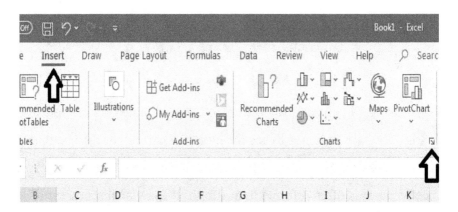

Fig 5: The **Insert** tab and **See All Charts** button indicated by the arrow

4. In the dialog box, click **All Charts** heading, select **Column** and click **Ok** button and the chart is inserted in the spreadsheet of excel.

Bar Chart

Bar chart is one of the easiest ways you can present your data in spreadsheet. A bar chart which is often referred to as bar graph represents a way which data can be represented in excel. They are used to display and compare numbers, frequency or other measures, for the different discrete categories of data.

How to Create Bar Chart in Excel

Bar chart can be created with the following steps:

1. Enter your data in the spreadsheet and select all the require data just as seen in the picture below:

54

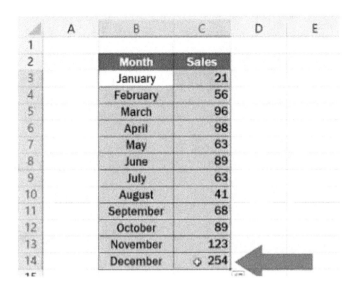

Fig 5.1: Selected data for bar chart

2. Click on the **Insert** tab and select **Recommend Chart** or **See All Charts** button if you are not working with newer excel version.

3. Click **All Charts** heading in the dialog box and select the **Bar** option. T

4. Select any bar chart style of your choice as shown below:

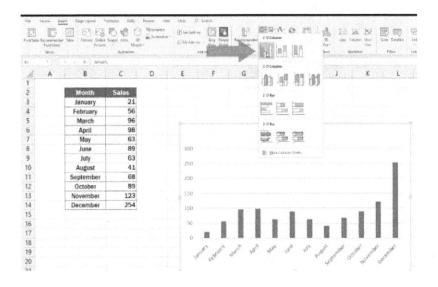

Fig 5.2: Select any bar chart style

5. Click **Ok** button and the chart is inserted in your spreadsheet.

How to Adjust the Position of the Graph within the Spreadsheet

The position of the graph within the spreadsheet can be adjusted in a very simple way. Click on the blank space within the chart area, hold the left button of your mouse and move the chart to any direction you want to place it.

How to Adjust the Size of the Graph in Excel

You can easily adjust the size of the graph by simply clicking at any corner area of the bar chart and drag it to any direction until the size of the graph is enough to your taste.

How to Add Graph Tittle in Excel

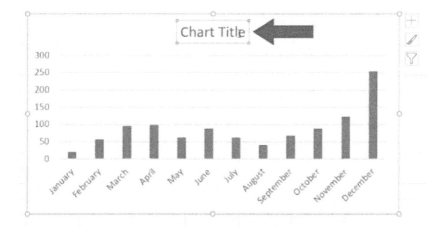

Fig 5.3: Graph title

You can name your graph anything you want. If you want to change the title name of your graph, just click on the caption and type in any name you want your graph to answer.

How to Change the Color and Design of a Graph

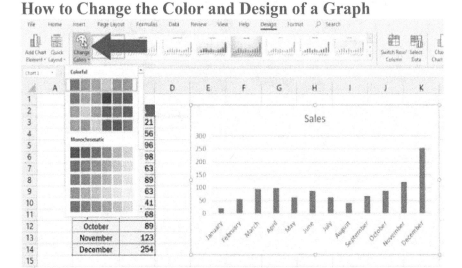

Fig 5.4: Changing graph color and design style

The color and the design of the graph can be changed according to your preference. To achieve this, click on the blank space of your chart area, go to Design tab and find the option "Change Colors" to pick a selection of color of your choice.

In addition, the whole graph design can be changed, go to Design tab again, look for Chart style and you will see a list of options to choose from. You can select any style of graph that you prefer in the available options.

How to make a Pie Chart in Excel

I will teach you how you can easily create pie chart in excel spreadsheet. Using a graph is a nice way to represent your data in effective virtual way. Using a well line graph in excel can make your data presentation clear and engaging. You can use your pie chart presentation to present your monthly sales. For example:

1. Select the area with available data like in the picture below. You can select all your data if you want your pie chart to represent all. Check the picture below.

	A	B	C	D	E
1					
2		Month	Sales		
3		January	21		
4		February	56		
5		March	96		
6		April	98		
7		May	63		
8		June	89		
9		July	63		
10		August	41		
11		September	68		
12		October	89		
13		November	123		
14		December	254		
15					

Fig 5.5: Selected data for pie chart

2. Once you are done making your selection, click on the **Insert** Tab.

3. Go to selection chart and select the **Pie** Chart option. They are several chart options you can choose from. I will pick the first one for the teaching. Immediately you click on the **Ok** button, the excel will immediately draw the chart and insert it in the spreadsheet. Our chart can be customized for on our own.

How to Change Color and Design of your Pie Chart
The color and design of your Pie Chart can be easily changed by clicking on the blank space area within your pie chart and click **Design**

tab. Find the option "**Change option**" and make selection of any color of your choice.

Introduction to Radar chart

In this subtopic, I will teach you how to create radar chart in excel. A radar chart compares the values of 3 or more variables relative to a central point. It is used when you cannot compare the variables directly and it is specially created for virtualizing performance and survey of data. Radar Chart design is used to show number of persons or the companies written along with several performance areas. Radar charts are also known as spider, web or star chart.

There are some typical usages of radar chart such as customer satisfaction survey, audit and inspection report.

However, for the better and more quickly to analyze the benefit and stability of a department, I think the radar chart can be a good choice.

How to Create Radar Chart

Creating a radar chart in excel is straightforward. You can create your radar chart by.

Step 1

Arrange your data in excel spreadsheet.

Step 2

Select the arranged data which you want to show in radar chart and click on **Insert** Tab.

Step 3

Click on **See All Charts** button

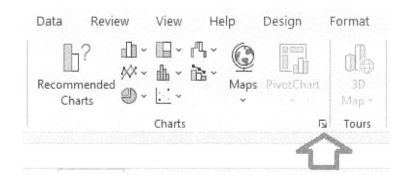

Fig 5.6: The See All Charts button pointed by the arrow

Step 4

In the dialog box, click the **All Charts** heading, select **Radar** and click **Ok** button for the chart to be inserted into spreadsheet.

Map Chart

You might be wondering what map chart is doing in excel. A map chart in excel can be used to compare values and show some categories across geographical regions. If you have some geographical regions in your workbook data, then you will have to use this chart to represent them, such as countries/regions, states, cities and their postal codes. With the map chart, you can represent different countries or locations in excel workbook in the form of map.

Example of How Data are Represent in the Map Chart

If you want to represent your data in a map chart, you will first organize the data you want to represent in the map and example is the one I have in the picture below.

	A	B	C	D
1	COUNTRIES	SALES IN USD		
2	UNITED KINGDOM	8000		
3	UNITED STATES	9000		
4	FRANCE	5700		
5	CANADA	6000		
6	JAPAN	3600		
7	GERMANY	6500		
8				

Fig 5.7: Arranged data for map chart

- Highlight the data which you entered in the spreadsheet.
- Click on **Insert** tab and click on the **See All Charts** button.
- Select All Charts heading in the dialog box.
- Select **Map** from the list of chart options and click **Ok** button for the chart to be inserted in your spreadsheet.

Make sure your computer is connected to internet before your map chart can be inserted successfully.

How to Adjust the Position of the Map Chart Within the Excel Spreadsheet

The chart in the spreadsheet can be position to any direction you want it to be. To do that, click on the blank space within the map chart area and hold the left mouse button and move the graph to any direction you want it to be.

How to Add Chart title in the Map Chart
You can name your map chart with any name you want. To do that, click on the caption **Title** and type in any name you want your Map graph to answer.

Histogram Chart Graph
A histogram chart is a type of chart that groups number into ranges. An excel histogram chart is easy to insert. Histogram chart is not often clear on when to make use of it or how to adjust it to the size you want it to be. This chart often looks like bar chart. A histogram chart is often used in frequency distribution of data with large value ranges.

In this teaching, I will show you how histogram chart can be set up. Take these steps to get the job done at the end.

1. Type in your data in the require cells and highlight the data just like the one in the picture below.

	Name	Entry Date	Yearly Salary
36			
37	Histogram to Analyze Salary Distribution		
38			
39	Name	Entry Date	Yearly Salary
40	Gary Mille	9/1/2006	60,270
41	James Wil	12/1/2009	39,627
42	Richard El	4/1/2016	29,727
43	Robert Sp	1/1/2005	93,668
44	Roger Mu	9/1/2011	134,000
45	Paul Gara	1/1/2005	34,808
46	Robert M	3/1/2017	134,468
47	Natalie Po	2/1/2019	45,000
48	Kim West	2/1/2014	89,500
49	Steele Bric	10/1/2011	21,972
50	Andre Coc	10/1/2011	80,000
51	Crystal De	12/1/2012	185,000
52	Robert M	10/1/2018	50,545
53	Daniel Gar	8/1/2004	140,000
54	Ann With	9/1/2001	100,000
55	Paul Hill	4/5/2006	68,357
56	Corinna Se	7/15/2010	46,055
57	Ewan Tho	9/1/2006	60,270

Fig 5.8: Highlighted data for histogram chart

2. Go to **Insert** tab. Click on **See All Charts** button, select **All Charts** heading and then **Histogram** chart from the list.

3. Click **Ok** button in the dialog box and the chart is inserted in your spreadsheet.

Changing Histogram Bin Size
You can change your histogram bin size as it is inserted in your spreadsheet. The picture explains something on that.

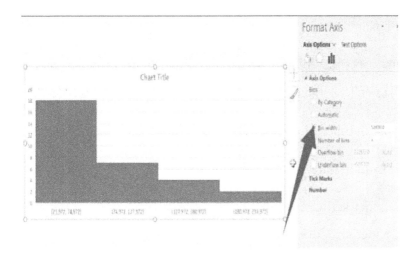

Fig 5.9: The histogram chart view

You can arrange your data histogram chart in different ranges and to do that press Ctrl + 1 and it will bring out the Format Axis options and select the bin width tab. You can change formula to any number you want, and it will take effect immediately on the histogram graph. You can as well define, overflow bin and underflow bin as well.

Printing in Excel

Printing in Excel is not a big task. I want to explain to you in detail about printing out excel document. I want to cover printing as its own topic because before you print out document, you need to format the data first so that your data will look more organized and professional when you print it out. If you are preparing your excel spreadsheet for printing purpose, that means this topic is for you but if you are not printing out your documents from your desktop computer, then skipping this topic will be best option but you can still go through it for more knowledge.

65

When you want to print, follow this guide:

1. In your worksheet, click **File** tab and select **Print** option. You can as well press Ctrl +P and it will take you to print preview window.

2. Enter the number of copies you want to print in the copies box.

3. Under printer, choose which printer to use.

4. Check under settings, choose what to print and configure the page margins, paper size, orientation etc.

5. Click the **Print** button.

Fig 5.1.1: Guide on printing in picture

Choose what to print: Print selection/ Active sheet/ Entire Workbook

If you want to tell excel what should be included in your printout, under the settings, click on the arrow next to print active sheets and select the following options

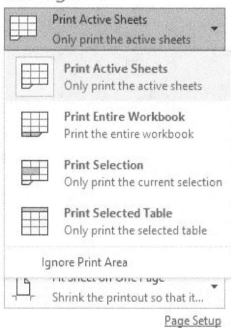

Fig 5.1.2: Setting the page print

The print selection allows you to print a highlight worksheet. To print only specific range of cell, what you need to do is to highlight it on the sheet, then choose print selection. To select nonadjacent cell, hold the **Ctrl** key during selection.

To print active sheets that you have open, you can select more than one worksheet by holding down your **Ctrl** key and then click on another worksheet name. Click on **Print Active Sheets**.

If you want to print multiple active sheets, click on the sheet tabs while you are still holding the **Ctrl** key and then choose **Print Active sheets**.

And to print the entire workbook, select **Print Entire Workbook**. And if you want to print out excel table, click any cell within your table, choose **Print Select Table**. Choosing to print more than one sheet at a time either using Entire workbook or Print Active Sheet, will result to strange thing happening to your headers and footers. For example, the page numbering will occur across worksheet. If you want your spreadsheet to look organized and standard, I will advise you print each documents data separately.

CHAPTER 6

MORE ON EXCEL AND FORMULAS

In this chapter, I will guide you further to understand the excel software. Also, I will guide you on the formulas and calculations in excel. Because this book is for beginners, I will concentrate on the basic operations. I will walk you through on addition, subtraction, multiplication and division.

The cell of Excel
Every spreadsheet in excel is made up of thousands of rectangular shapes which are called cells. The cells are the intersection between rows and columns. Columns are the ones that have identity of alphabets such as A, B, C on them. While rows are the ones with 1, 2, 3... on them. Each cell has its own identity name based on its column and row.

For example:

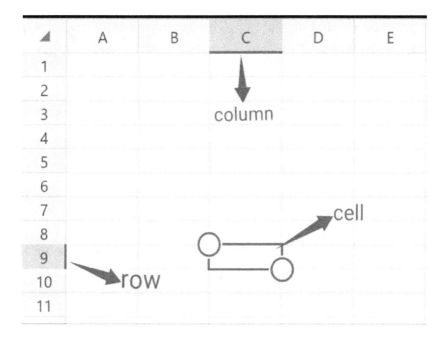

Fig 6: View of row, cell and column

- The C1 means that the number is in column C row number 1.
- The C8 means that the number is in column C row number 8.
- The B2 means to that the number is in column B row number 2.
- The A4 Means that the number is in column A row number 4.
- The E10 means that the number is in column E row number 10.

Arithmetic operators in Excel

Arithmetic operators in Excel specify the calculation you want to perform to give you the required result you want. Arithmetic operators are used to do some calculations such as addition (+), subtraction (-), multiplication (*) and division (/). This set of operators are used in numerical calculations.

Basic Excel Formulas Guide

To master the basic Excel formulas as a beginner will help you to know how to sum and calculate your work in excel spreadsheet. Microsoft Excel is considered the industry standard piece of software in data analysis. A formula in excel is an expression that returns specific results. Formula is very important in excel. It is mathematical calculation of data to give a result. Microsoft spreadsheet program is one of the preferred software by investment bankers and financial analysts in data processing and financial modelling. I will try my possible best to explain some basic parts to you.

Function and Formulas in Excel

We are going to use this sample of formulas to practice on the function and formulas in excel.

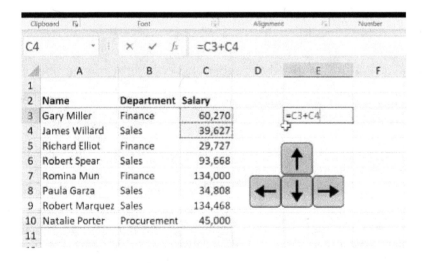

Fig 6.1: Prepared data

In the above data, we have Name, Department and Salary. In Excel, when you want to type in your formula, you are to start with equals sign (=) first just like the one shown above figure beside the major data.

	A	B	C	D	E
1	Add	3	6	9	
2	Subtract	15	3	12	
3	Multiply	12	2	24	
4	Divide	24	2	12	
5					
6					

Fig 6.2: Prepared data for major operators' calculations

To add up formula in excel spreadsheet you are to follow some steps. In the above prepared prepared table, I have calculated all the required answer in Column D. I will show you how I got all the required answer in the table.

For Addition

One of the simplest ways in adding up values in Excel is by:

- Preparing your data.
- Select the cell you want your answer value to be placed.
- Type in the column name and row number as I explained before. For example, in my prepared table, the data I wanted

to sum up is in column B and C, in row number 1. So, I typed **=B1+C1** and hit Enter key to get result.

Another way to Add up Data

One of the easiest ways you can add up formula in Excel is to use **AutoSum** command. Take these steps to add values using the command:

- Prepare the data you want to sum up in the spreadsheet.
- Select the numbers.
- Click on the **Formula** tab.
- Click on the **AutoSum** command and select Sum among the options shown to you.

Subtraction

Subtraction is another basic operator in Mathematics. I this section, I will guide you on how to subtract values in excel.

To subtract values in excel, take these steps:

- Prepare the data you will like to subtract in a spreadsheet.
- Select the cell where you want your answer to be inserted.
- Type in the column name with row number and subtract it with the column name with row number on the cell you want your answer to be inserted.

For example, type **=B2-C2** and hit Enter key of your keyboard for the answer to show up. I inserted the formula **=B2-C2** in the cell where I needed an answer before hitting Enter key and that was how I got the answer **12** in Fig 6.2.

Multiplication

To do multiplication of data in your formula,

- Prepare your data.
- Select the cell you want your answer to be inserted.
- Introduce = sign, type in the column letter with the row number and multiply it with the column letter and row number of the other.
- Press Enter key of the computer keyboard.

For example, from Fig 6.2, to get my data multiplied, I typed =**B3*C3** and pressed the Enter key.

Division in Excel

To carryout division of data in excel, the steps you need to take are as follow:

- Prepare your data first.
- Select the cell you want the answer to be inserted.
- Introduce = sign, type the column name with the row number slash with the column name with row number of the one to divide.

For example, in Fig 6.2, to get my data divided, I typed =**B4/C4** and pressed Enter key.

Sum Function

Sum function is used in adding up all the number in excel spreadsheet. This is another method of carrying out addition in excel. It is another formula you can apply to add numbers and get the exact result.

To use sum function, these are the steps to follow:

- Prepare your data
- Select the cell you want your answer to be inserted
- Type in =SUM(Inside the parenthesis, highlight all the required numbers you want to sum up).
- After the closure of parenthesis, press the Enter key to give you result.

For example, the picture below explains the Mathematics.

C11		× ✓ ƒx	=SUM(C3:C10)	
	A	B	C	D
1				
2	Name	Department	Salary	
3	Gary Miller	Finance	60,270	
4	James Willard	Sales	39,627	
5	Richard Elliot	Finance	29,727	
6	Robert Spear	Sales	93,668	
7	Romina Mun	Finance	134,000	
8	Paula Garza	Sales	34,808	
9	Robert Marquez	Sales	134,468	
10	Natalie Porter	Procurement	45,000	
11			=SUM(C3:C10)	
12				

Fig 6.3: Use of SUM function in picture

Finding Average Value in Excel
You can find the average of the numbers you have inserted in cells.

To find the average value in the range of cells, used an average function. To get the average of a function in range data, follow the below steps:

- Prepare your data. You can look at the one I prepared in Fig 6.3.

- Click on empty cell where you want your answer to be placed.

- Highlight the cells you want to find the average and click on the **Formula** tab.

- Click on the AutoSum command and click on the **Average**.

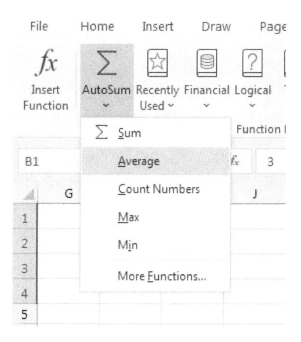

Fig 6.4: Finding the average of numbers

You can as well input average formula directly to excel sheet by the following ways:

- After you have prepared your data, select the cell where you want your data answer to be.

- Type =average open bracket, select the cells with the numbers you want to find the average, close the bracket and press Enter key.

Minimum

To find the minimum value in a range of cells, you can use minimum function. To find the minimum value in a prepared data, follow the below steps:

- Select the numbers in the range of cells.
- Click on the **Formulas** tab.
- Click on the **AutoSum** and select **Min** among the options.

Maximum

To find the highest value in a range of cells, use maximum function. The maximum tool in the Formula tab gives you the maximum number you want to get from your prepare data. To perform the task of finding maximum value, follow these steps:

- Select the cells that contains the number you wish to find the maximum value from.
- Click on the **Formulas** tab
- Click on the **AutoSum** command and select **Max**.

Count Numbers in Cells

The count number counts the number of cells in range that contains numbers. If you want to count number of your data in cells, type in =count (in this bracket, highlight all the required range) and press Enter key.

Can Count Number Function Also Count Name?

No! The count number function only counts numbers not names or letters. If you want to count text, you will have to use different options called CountA function.

CountA Function Explained

If you want to count text in your prepared table, you need to use countA function. The CountA function counts the number of cells in a range that are not empty. This CountA function does not care if its number or text that is in a cell. To take up the task, type =CountA (highlight the cells which contains the names and numbers you want to count) and press Enter key. The picture below shows where CountA function is used.

SUM	⌄ :	✕ ✓	fx	=COUNTa(A3:A10)

◢	A	B		
1			ⓕCOUNTA Counts the n	
			ⓕDCOUNTA	
2	Name	Department	Salary	
3	Gary Miller	Finance	60,270	
4	James Willard	Sales	39,627	
5	Richard Elliot	Finance	29,727	
6	Robert Spear	Sales	93,668	
7	Romina Mun	Finance	134,000	
8	Paula Garza	Sales	34,808	
9	Robert Marquez	Sales	134,468	
10	Natalie Porter	Procurement	45,000	
11		Sum	571,568	
12		Average	71,446	
13		Count salary	8	
14		Count names	=COUNTa(	

Fig 6.5: CountA function in picture

Using the FX Command in Formulas Tab

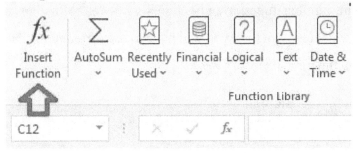

Fig 6.6: FX command indicated by the arrow

Excel have different form of functions. You can find a function by clicking on FX button in the spreadsheet of Excel. This FX function is often located at the left of the formula bar. By default, the Insert function dialog lists the most recently used functions.

All the Excel's functions are categorized into the following categories: Financial, Date & Time, Math & Trig, Statistical, Lookup & Reference, Database, Text, Logical, Information, Cube, and Engineering. It can be difficult to correctly guess the category.

SUM is a Math & Trig function, yet AVERAGE is a Statistical function. Rather than browse each category, you can type few words in the search box and click Go. Excel will show you the relevant functions to choose from.

Excel on Mobile
To be able to use Excel application in your Mobile phones, you are to download it from Playstore using an android phone or Appstore if you are using iPhone. In the beginning of this book, I have explained to you how you can download and install it on your mobile phone. It is

time to know how you can operate the excel which you have downloaded in your mobile phone.

How You can Operate Excel on Your Phone

After you have downloaded the Excel application in your mobile phone, the next thing you need to do, is to click on the Excel app which you downloaded, and it will open showing something like this.

Fig 6.7: The mobile excel view

To start the work on your workbook, click on the (+) sign and it will take you to another page, then click on the Blank workbook to open a blank excel worksheet.

How to Enter Data in the Blank Workbook

If you have not used excel in your phone, to enter text in the cell can be confusing. If you click on the cell once, it may not allow you to enter any text at first. If you have that experience, before you can enter text in the cell, you will double-click on it.

Creating a Chart with Excel on a Mobile Device

To insert chart on your mobile phone's excel, you have to follow the steps below:

- Open your blank workbook and prepare your data which you want to use to prepare your chart.

- Drag the handle to select the data you want to include in your chart.

- Tap on the drop-down button which is located at the right-hand side of the interface to be able to view some tools.

Fig 6.8: Steps in selecting Insert tab for chart creation

- When you click on the drop-down button, it will show up **Home** tab, tap on the Home tab which is located at the left-hand corner of the page.

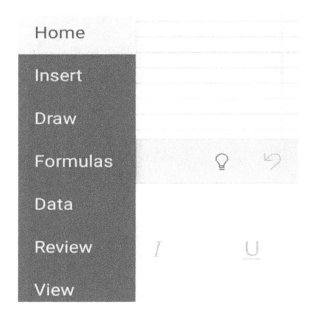

Fig 6.9: Select Insert tab from the list

- Click on the **Insert** tab.
- You will be shown some commands in the Insert tab. Click on the **Chart** command, select the kind of chart you want, and it is inserted in the spreadsheet.

How to Save File Using Excel Mobile App

Saving of documents is enabled in Excel mobile application. You can give your file a unique name of your choice. To do that, follow the steps below:

- After you have finished preparing your data, you can save it up by clicking at the ellipsis (the three dots located at right-hand of the workbook).

Fig 6.1.1: Step in saving your excel document file on mobile

- At the options which will show up after you have click on ellipsis, tap on the **Save As** button.
- Type in the name you want your documents to answer in the space provided.
- Tap at the place you want your file to be saved in your mobile phone. If you want your document to be saved on your mobile, click on the **This Device** tab. Or you can save your document on OneDrive by clicking on OneDrive option.
- Click on **Save** button to save.

Sharing Files Using Excel Mobile App
Files can as well be shared through mobile excel application. To be able to share file using excel mobile, follow below steps:

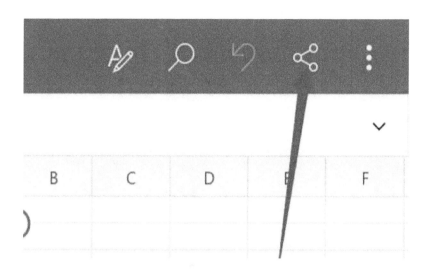

Fig 6.1.1: Share icon indicated

- Click on the **Share** icon on the right-hand corner of the app interface.

- Click the tab where you want your file to be shared, either with OneDrive or Share as attachment, and provide other information required such as the email of the person you are sending the file to.

INDEX

M

map chart, *61, 62*
maximum, *29, 78*
minimum, *29, 78*
multiplication, 70, 72, 75

O

OneDrive, *38, 39, 42, 84, 85*

P

paste, *7, 21, 46*
pie chart, *58*
Print Entire Workbook, *69*
Print Select Table, *69*
printing, *65, 67*
Protect Workbook, *52*

Q

quick access toolbar, *32, 39*

R

radar chart, *60*
review tab, *34, 48, 49*
Row, *6*

S

save, 18, 31, 39, 41, 42, 83, 84
Saving and sharing, *38*
sheet name, *46*
smart lookup, *49*
Subtraction, 74

T

template, *10, 18*
terminologies, *5*
Thesaurus, *48, 49*
translate, *50*

U

underline, *21, 22*

V

view tab, *34*

W

Workbook Statistics, *49*
wrap text, *26*
Wrap Text, *26*

This is a well written book by a professional in software and usage. There are many things you will learn from this book on excel. Among what you will learn are:
Why you need to learn how to use excel software
Fundamentals in excel
Formatting in excel spreadsheet
How to edit in spreadsheet
Excel Formulas and functions
How to create different kinds of charts and many more.

ISBN 9798748287098

90000

9 798748 287098